BONGA BONGA
& GRANDPA

A Fish Story

GEOFFREY B. HADDAD
with *Bonga Bonga*

 FriesenPress

Suite 300 - 990 Fort St
Victoria, BC, V8V 3K2
Canada

www.friesenpress.com

ISBN
978-1-5255-2760-9 (Hardcover)
978-1-5255-2761-6 (Paperback)
978-1-5255-2762-3 (eBook)

1. *JUVENILE NONFICTION, SCIENCE & NATURE, ZOOLOGY*
2. *JUVENILLE NON-FICTION, FAMILY, MULTIGENERATIONAL*
3. *JUVENILLE NON-FICTION, ANIMALS, FISH*

Distributed to the trade by The Ingram Book Company

AUTHOR'S NOTE

– Through the years with Bonga Bonga –

Through the Years with Bonga Bonga is a series of true and educational children's stories, covering a wide range of topics. Inspired by the love of a grandfather for his first grandchild, affectionately known as Bonga Bonga, these delightful tales will make excellent additions to personal and school libraries alike.

Although the stories are mostly the work of Grandpa, they are written from Bonga Bonga's perspective. The narrative will engage and entertain readers of all ages.

Bonga Bonga and Grandpa covers the period from when Bonga Bonga was one to eight years old. *Bonga Bonga and Grandpa—A Fish Story* is the first in the series.

I hope you enjoy this book, and the many more to come, with your children and grandchildren.

For **Bonga Bonga,**
With all my love,
Grandpa

My Dear Grandpa,

I want to thank you so very much for writing these lovely stories about us.

I will always remember and treasure them, especially all the fun times we had together.

I wish that all of the children in the world could have a grandpa like you.

With all my love,
Your Bonga Bonga

HOW I GOT MY NAME

When I was about six months old, my mummy and daddy bought me a play mat with some toys hanging from the frame over my head. My favourite one was the monkey. He was always dangling his feet in my face. Whenever he did that, I would pull on them and he would say "**Bonga Bonga**."

My grandpa says that is how
I got my special name ...
Bonga Bonga.

Dedicated to

Isabella Rachel, Julianna Sarah, Evelyn Grace,

and

Jonah Zachariah—

the joys of my life.

FOR GRANDCHILDREN—

"When you are young,
your grandparents try to tell you
their history,
and you don't care because
it doesn't interest you at the time.
Later on, you wish you had written
what they said down".

—*Lillian Trujillo*

FOR PARENTS AND GRANDPARENTS—

"An excerpt from *On Children*"

"Your children are not your children.
They are the sons and daughters of Life's longing
for itself.
They come through you but not from you,
And though they are with you yet they belong not
to you.

You may give them your love but not your thoughts,
For they have their own thoughts.
You may house their bodies but not their souls,
For their souls dwell in the house of tomorrow,
which you cannot visit, not even in your dreams.
You may strive to be like them,
but seek not to make them like you.
For life goes not backward nor tarries
with yesterday."

By Kahlil Gibran

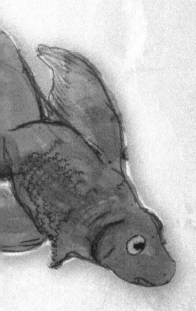

THE FISH

My grandpa told me that when he was a little boy, around eight years old, he did many things after school. He had a lot of fun playing sports. Grandpa made planes and boats and kites. But most of all, Grandpa liked keeping fish. He had many glass jars and small aquariums filled with different types of fish.

THE MUMMY & DADDY FISH

My grandpa said that the mummy and daddy fish decided to have babies. Some of the mummy fish had babies by laying eggs. The eggs took a few days to hatch into babies.

Other ones had babies come out of their mummy's tummy, like I did. Those babies would swim around right away.

Soon all of my grandpa's glass jars and aquariums were filled with mummy and daddy fish. They were of all sorts, and there were lots and lots of baby fish too.

My grandpa did not have anywhere else to put more glass jars or aquariums. He had no idea what to do, but he wanted to keep all of his beautiful fish ... and even have more, if he could.

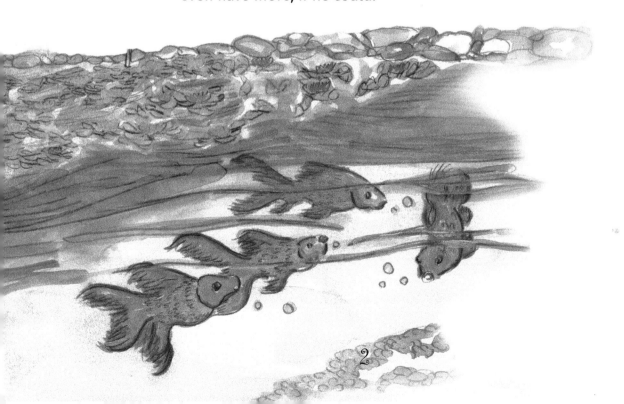

THE FISH PONDS

My grandpa said that when he was ten years old, his daddy took him to the pet store. He asked the owner what he should do. The owner told my grandpa how to build fish ponds in his back garden. The ponds could be made out of blocks and concrete. Concrete is made from cement, stones, sand, and water. Grandpa could make the ponds as big as he wanted to. He could even build as many ponds as his daddy said he could. He could also have as many fish as he wanted. My grandpa said that this made him very excited.

But how would he get the money to buy blocks and all the things he needed to make concrete? And when would he have the time to build the ponds in his back garden?

My grandpa thought and thought for a very long time, and finally he got some ideas. He first decided that he would eat all of his meals at home—even if he did not like them. That way, he would not have to spend all of the money that his daddy gave him to buy lunch at school.

Grandpa also said that his daddy always came late to pick him up after school, so he decided to stay in his classroom and do his homework before going home. That way, he could work on his ponds when he got home. Most of Grandpa's school friends stayed after school so that they could play. They played soccer, tennis, marbles, and hopscotch. He always wanted to play too, but he remembered the fun he had with his fish.

4

After six months, Grandpa had saved enough money to build a pond in his back garden. It was as big as my play pool, except it was not round.

Grandpa said that he made the walls with blocks and the bottom with concrete. He also used the concrete to join the blocks together to make the walls. And soon he built more ponds.

My grandpa was so happy to put all the fish from the glass jars and aquariums into the ponds. He had a pond for each type of fish, 'ecause some of the fish did not like the other fish. They would often fight and sometimes eat or kill each other.

My grandpa's daddy and mummy were also very happy, 'ecause my grandpa did all of his homework before coming home. Also, my grandpa ate all of his meals and even asked for more … most of the time.

After many years, my grandpa had more than ten ponds and fifteen types of fish. The ponds were all filled with fish.

Grandpa told me that in the fish world, the daddy ones are more beautiful than the mummy ones, but I did not tell that to my mummy or my grandma!

My grandpa's favourite fish were:

The **zebra** fish. These fish have black stripes, just like the **zebras** found mainly in Africa. The **tiger barb** fish also have stripes, just like the **tigers** that are also found mainly in Africa.

His other favourites were the **platties** - sometimes red and orange, and black mollies. They almost look the same except for their colours.

Next came the **gouramis**. I do not know how to say that name correctly, so I just say "grammies." My grandpa always says it correctly for me. Some of them are **blue** and the others **pink**. Grandpa told me that they both have feelers, or whiskers, like his and Grandma's kittens, Moo Moo and Candy Brandy.

The **pink** ones ... well, they are really different, 'ecause they have funny lips. When they fight, the daddy ones use their lips. They are not actually kissing, but fighting.

The next ones were the **Siamese** fighting fish, also called Betta Fish. Those were my grandpa's special ones! The daddy ones are very, very pretty.

Then came the **goldfish**.

JAMAICA

My grandpa lived on the tiny island of Jamaica. Jamaica is about five thousand miles away from Vancouver, Canada. Grandpa said that you have to take two jet planes, and it takes almost twelve hours, to go from Jamaica to Vancouver.

In Jamaica, it is very hot most of the time. It also rains a lot, and sometimes there are hurricanes.

Sometimes it would rain so much, my grandpa's ponds would overflow. Some of the fish would swim into his mummy's flower gardens. Grandpa would use his net to catch them and put them back in the ponds. His net looked very much like the one I use to catch butterflies.

Another problem was the neighbour's kitty, Mittens. She was a rude cat. She would sometimes drink water from the ponds, and sometimes she ate Grandpa's fish.

There was another problem—dragonflies. They would lay their eggs in Grandpa's ponds. The babies are called nymphs and look like small frogs. They loved to eat his baby fish.

But my grandpa was very smart. He put some wire mesh—like the kind he used to make cages for his guinea pigs, rabbits, and birds—over the ponds. Neither Mittens nor the dragonfly nymphs ever ate his fish again.

All of Grandpa's fish were tropical fish, and they liked warm water.

Grandpa told me that he had nearly a thousand fish. That's heaps of fish!

My grandpa said that he often dreamed of the day he could have one large pond with a river running into it.

That was a long time ago.

THE GARDEN POND

Shortly after my grandpa finished his studies at university, he moved to West Vancouver, in Canada. This is where I live. One day, my grandpa got an idea to build a huge pond in the back garden of his home. He decided to make the pond in the shape of his homeland, Jamaica.

Grandpa worked very hard with some workmen and built a large pond in his back garden.

It was two feet deep in the middle and held lots of water. I think it held fifteen hundred gallons. That's lots and lots and lots of water!

The pond had a fountain in the middle and lights all around. Grandpa also put lights under the water. He put some small white pebbles and some white sand at one edge of the pond. He told me that it was to remind him of the beautiful, sandy white beaches in his homeland of Jamaica.

Grandpa also built a river running into his fish pond and a waterfall on the river. The river was about twenty feet long.

His dream had come true.

But Grandpa knew he had a problem. He could not keep all those beautiful, tropical fish in Vancouver. For one thing, the water was too cold in winter. Also, my grandpa thought that his tropical fish could only breathe by swimming to the top of the water to get air. He knew that in the winter in Vancouver, the water at the top of the pond would become ice. He worried that the fish would die, 'ecause they would not be able to get to the top of the water to breathe.

My grandpa became very sad. He wished that he could find some fish that could live in the very cold water under the ice in his pond. *What fish could those be?* he thought to himself. *What fish could do that?*

THE GOLDFISH

Grandpa said that one day he asked the owner of the pet store in Vancouver what type of fish could live in very cold water without coming to the top to breathe. He was surprised to learn that **goldfish** could survive in very cold water and could breathe without using oxygen. They didn't have to come to the top. But the owner of the pet store did not tell Grandpa why, 'ecause he did not know! They could stay under water all the time!

Now my grandpa was worried about how to feed the **goldfish** when winter came and the pond was covered with ice. The owner of the pet store told him not to worry. He said that **goldfish** were like polar bears in the winter. They moved very little and slept a lot. They also ate very little. The **goldfish** could also get enough food in the winter by eating some moss and weeds at the bottom of the pond.

Soon afterwards, my grandpa became so happy that he went to the pet store and bought all kinds of **goldfish**.

Some of the **goldfish** were red, some white, and some red and white. Others had tails

that looked like a fan. He said that those were Fantail Goldfish. There were some black ones with large eyes that also had fantails. Those were called **Black Moors**.

My grandpa told me that, at first, he had about fifty goldfish, and he would feed them from his bench by the pond once a day.

Some of my grandpa's friends told him that Ronnie and his family of **raccoons** would come and eat his goldfish.

Grandpa went to the pet store, and the owner told him that he should place some chemicals called white moth balls around the pond. This would stop Ronnie and his family of **raccoons** from coming.

Now Grandpa was worried about the chemicals, 'ecause of his and Grandma's two cats, Moo Moo and Candy Brandy. What if Moo Moo and Candy Brandy ate those white moth balls? They worried especially about Moo Moo, 'ecause he was always hungry and would eat all the leftovers on my tray table—mostly when I was sleeping. But Moo Moo and Candy Brandy were smart cats and stayed far away from those white moth balls.

Ronnie and his family of **raccoons** never came either!

After a while, Grandpa became so happy with his goldfish and pond that he went to the pet store and bought some more. He was so happy that no **raccoons** had come, 'ecause he had placed the white moth balls around the pond.

THE HERON

A few months after he had placed the white moth balls around the pond, Grandpa went to see owner of the pet store and looked sad.

"What is the matter?" the owner asked.

"Someone has stolen all of my goldfish, and I do not know who," Grandpa said.

"I have a good idea of who did it, and we can make sure it does not happen again," said the owner of the pet store.

"But what could that be?" Grandpa asked.

"You see, Mr. H., there is a big bird that flies high over your house each day on its way to catch fish from the sea. He also flies over your house at night on his way back home. That bird is called a heron, and he can see your little goldfish from high in the sky. He is the one stealing and eating your fish," the owner said to my grandpa.

"But how can I stop him from eating my goldfish?" Grandpa asked.

"Here, Mr. H., this is a plastic heron that looks just like the real heron. Put it at the edge of your pond. Herons do not like to be near other herons when it is time to eat. When the real heron sees your plastic heron, he will just fly over your house and not eat your goldfish."

Grandpa hurried home with the plastic heron and stuck it in the ground near to the edge of his pond.

He then bought around twenty goldfish and put them in his pond. My grandpa was once again happy.

Five days later, Grandpa could only count ten goldfish.

"What could have happened to some of my goldfish?" he shouted.

MR. BROWN - THE CARPENTER

"I saw him eating them," Grandpa's neighbour, Mr. Brown, answered. "The **heron** was in your pond last night eating your **goldfish**."

Grandpa was so sad and upset, 'ecause the **heron** had again eaten his **goldfish**.

"Now what should I do?" Grandpa said to Mr. Brown.

"Do not worry, Mr. H., I am a carpenter. I will help you build a net over your pond. That **heron** will never eat your **goldfish** again."

The next day, Mr. Brown and my grandpa started to work on a huge net on a metal frame. After it was done, they celebrated ... and Grandpa bought some more **goldfish**.

GRANDPA'S GARDEN AND POND

Many months went by. On my first birthday, Grandpa showed me his beautiful garden and the pond he had built. He said that he and Grandma were the gardeners, but that he alone was in charge of the goldfish and the pond.

I enjoyed playing in my grandpa and grandma's back garden. I would sometimes chase bubbles, splash in my pool, play with Moo Moo and Candy Brandy, and just run around. It was such fun.

My grandpa sometimes let me feed the goldfish and play with them. Sometimes he would catch the goldfish and pet them. At times, the goldfish would get stuck in the net, and I would help my grandpa put them back in the pond.

When I was a little older, my grandpa would let me throw stones in the river near the waterfall. Grandpa also planted some sweet-smelling grass near the waterfalls. I would rub the back of my hands on this grass, and it smelled just like mint.

My grandpa also put some of my plastic toy ducks, daddies and mummies and some baby ones too, in his pond.

Whenever I visited my grandpa, the first thing we did was collect the fish food and the net. Then off we would go to sit on the bench by the pond.

My grandpa made his own fish food. I think he made it mostly of oats—the kind that Grandma used to make porridge for me. My grandpa crushed the oats into tiny pieces in his hand so that the goldfish could eat them, 'ecause goldfish do not have teeth like me, or my mummy and daddy, or my grandpa and my grandma.

Next, we would rescue any fish stuck in the net, and I would throw them back in the pond. Once one was stuck in the net for too long and it died. I cried a bit, but my grandpa told me not to worry, 'ecause the mummy goldfish had just had five baby ones. They would soon grow to be big goldfish.

After I threw stones in the river, Grandpa let me sail pieces of sticks or leaves down the river, and I would watch them go over the waterfalls.

Next, I would pull the toy ducks—the mummy and daddy ones, and the baby ones too—out of the water and onto the grass and play with them.

MY MINGO

When I was older, Grandpa was so happy, 'ecause no **herons** or **raccoons** had stolen any of his goldfish for a long time. He was so happy that he bought another plastic **heron** from the owner of the pet store, but this time he made it into a flamingo.

He painted the flamingo pink to remind me of the flamingos we saw in Mexico. I called the flamingo "My Mingo," and I kept him in my grandpa's basement.

Each time I'd visit my grandpa, he would ask me to stand on one leg, just like "My Mingo." That always made us laugh.

21

THE BIRDS AND THE BIRDFEEDER

In the summertime I would help my grandpa feed the birds. We fed them different types of bird feed, like the kinds we used to feed the ducks sometimes.

The tree with the birdfeeder was at one end of Grandpa's pond. The birds would first perch in the maple tree before going to the birdfeeder.

We put the bird feed in the little house. The birds were mostly blue birds called Steller's jay, not the blue jays.

THE EMPTY BENCH & POND

In the spring of 2012, when I was three years old, I visited my grandpa and saw him looking very sad in his rocking chair.

"What is the matter, Grandpa?" I asked.

He held my hand as we walked toward the river, the waterfall, and the pond.

When we got to the pond, Grandpa sat me on the bench beside him and asked me to look in the pond.

I saw why my Grandpa was sad, and I also became sad and wanted to cry.

The goldfish had once again gone from the pond. Ronnie and his **raccoon** family had ripped the net over the pond, and the heron had come and eaten all of our goldfish. The last time we counted, we had seventy-two goldfish.

My grandpa hugged me tightly, and I promised that I would not cry.

"Do not worry, Bonga Bonga," he said.

I tried not to, but I cried a little.

"Mr. Brown has a new plan for the heron and the **raccoons**. Soon we will have lots of goldfish once again."

I felt happy as my grandpa wiped the tears from my cheek.

Then we ran into the front yard and started flying the kite my grandpa had made for me.

Soon after grandpa and Mr. Brown put some lights, some things that spewed out water, and some things that made loud noises around his pond. I did not understand it all, but it scared the herons and Ronnie and his raccoon family. They never came again!

Then my grandpa and me bought some more goldfish. And we were very happy once again.